W9-BHG-332

SOUTHERN COOKING

Designed by Claire Leighton
Recipe photography by Peter Barry
Recipes styled by Bridgeen Deery and Wendy Devenish
Edited by Jillian Stewart

CLB 2810
© 1992 Colour Library Books Ltd, Godalming, Surrey, England.
All rights reserved.
This 1992 edition published by Crescent Books,
distributed by Outlet Book Company Inc., a Random House Company,
40 Engelhard Avenue, Avenel, New Jersey 07001.
Printed and bound in Singapore.
ISBN 0 517 06604 1
8 7 6 5 4 3 2 1

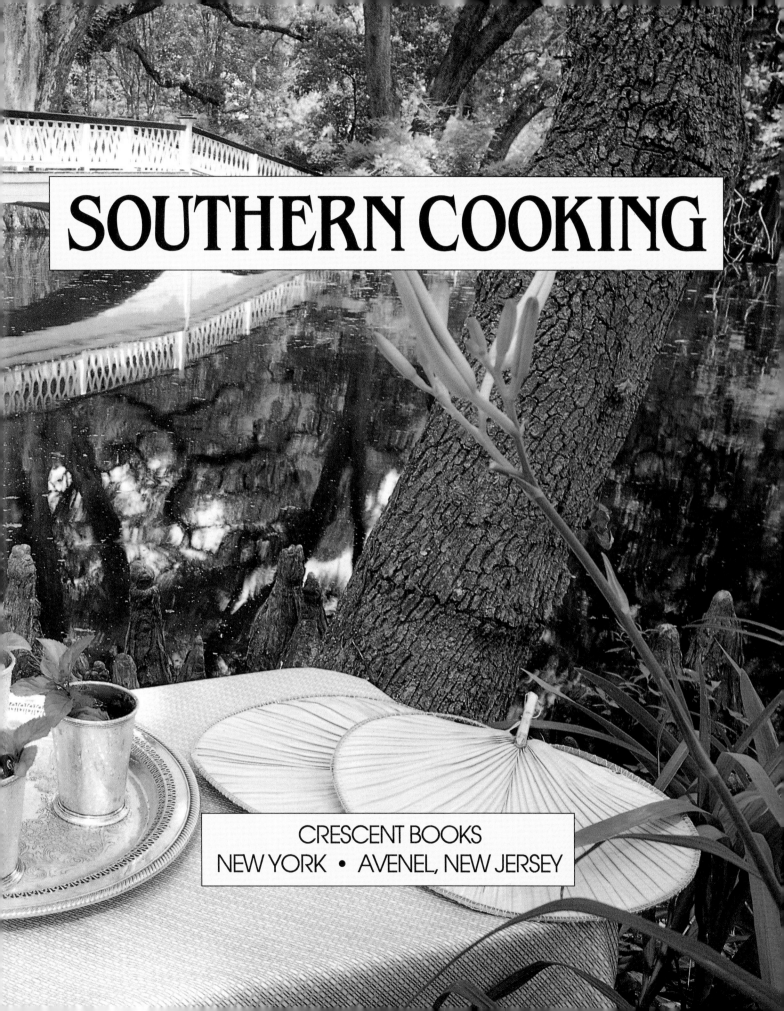

SOUTHERN COOKING

CRESCENT BOOKS
NEW YORK • AVENEL, NEW JERSEY

INTRODUCTION

Southern hospitality is famous throughout the United States and beyond. And the South's reputation for warmth, friendliness and sheer hospitality is wonderfully reflected in the food of the region. The roots of Southern cooking, like most regional cooking styles, are based on the local produce, the climate, and the culture of the people themselves.

The ethnic mix of the South has greatly affected its distinctive cuisine, which shows the unmistakable influence of its French, Spanish and African heritage. Once famous in history for its gracious living, elegant plantation houses and lavish entertaining, the South is also known for its farming heritage, with its hearty, delicious fare made up of whatever the cook had on hand. Each region of the South does of course have its specialties, all with their own particular style, yet all particularly American.

Louisiana brings us two of the South's best loved styles – Cajun and Creole. Cajun cooking originated in the swamps and bayous, whereas Creole cooking is centered in New Orleans. Both styles owe something to classic French cuisine, while utilizing local produce such as spices, peppers, rice and seafood.

Alabama is responsible for one of those indisputable Southern favorites, fried chicken. And who could forget wonderful baked ham given a new twist with a sweet cola glaze. Tennessee also has its favorites. Once a wild frontier, it is the home of some real down-home Southern cooking, with muffins and biscuits that simply can't be beaten.

Some of the loveliest landscapes in the United States are to be found in the bluegrass state of Kentucky, land of the Derby and of that most famous Southern refreshment, the mint julep. Kentucky was also home to the Shakers, who prided themselves on using local ingredients in ways that were unpretentious, yet tasty and imaginative.

Florida instantly brings to mind beaches with fine, white sand, but the state also boasts beautiful old cities as well as the natural beauty of the mysterious Everglades. Seafood is one of its greatest natural bounties and the inspiration for some of the most wonderful recipes to be found anywhere in the South.

Only a few of the Southern states are mentioned here, but wherever you go in the region you will find a welcome that is legendary and wonderful local cuisine that is difficult to surpass.

Right: Agrirama, the living history museum in Tifton, Louisiana, is a celebration of farming during the late nineteenth century. Traditional Southern field crops such as corn, cotton and tobacco are grown just as they would have been in the 1890s.

Virginia Peanut Soup

Preparation Time: 15 minutes **Cooking Time:** 15 minutes **Serves:** 4

Peanuts, popular all over the South, make a velvety rich soup that is easily made from ordinary store cupboard ingredients.

Ingredients

4 tbsps butter or margarine
2 tbsps flour
1 cup creamy peanut butter
¼ tsp celery seed

2½ cups chicken stock
½ cup dry sherry
½ cup coarsely chopped peanuts

Melt the butter or margarine in a medium saucepan. Remove from the heat and stir in the flour. Add the peanut butter and celery seed. Gradually pour on the stock, stirring constantly. Return the pan to the heat and simmer gently for about 15 minutes. Do not allow to boil rapidly. Stir in the sherry and ladle into a tureen or individual bowls. Sprinkle with the chopped peanuts.

A reconstruction of a pioneer house at Pioneer Village, Noccalula Falls Park, Alabama.

Corn and Potato Chowder

Preparation Time: 25 minutes **Cooking Time:** 25-30 minutes **Serves:** 6-8

Such a filling soup, this is really a complete meal in a bowl. Corn is a favorite ingredient in Southern cooking.

Ingredients

6 medium potatoes, peeled
Chicken or vegetable stock
1 onion, finely chopped
2 tbsps butter or margarine
4oz cooked ham, chopped
1 tbsp flour

4 ears fresh corn or about
  4oz canned corn
3 cups milk
Salt and dash of Tabasco
Finely chopped parsley

Quarter the potatoes and place them in a deep saucepan. Add stock to cover and the onion, and bring the mixture to the boil. Lower the heat and simmer, partially covered, until the potatoes are soft – about 15-20 minutes. Drain the potatoes, reserving ¾ pint of the cooking liquid. Mash the potatoes and combine with reserved liquid.

Melt the butter or margarine in a clean pan, add the ham and cook briefly. Stir in the flour and pour over the potato mixture, mixing well.

If using fresh corn, remove the husks and silk and, holding one end of the corn, stand the ear upright. Use a large sharp knife and cut against the cob vertically from top to bottom just scraping off the kernals. Add the corn and milk to the potato mixture and bring almost to the boil. Do not boil the corn rapidly as this will toughen it. Add a pinch of salt and a dash of Tabasco, and garnish with parsley before serving.

She Crab Soup

Preparation Time: 35-40 minutes **Cooking Time:** 25 minutes **Serves:** 4

A female crab, with roe intact, is needed for a truly authentic soup. However, an ordinary crab can be used and the result will be just as delicious.

Ingredients

1 large crab, cooked	6 tbsps sherry
3 tbsps butter or margarine	Pinch salt, white pepper and
1 onion, very finely chopped	ground mace
2 tbsps flour	½ cup heavy cream, whipped
4 cups milk	Red caviar

To dress the crab, take off all the legs and the large claws. Crack the large claws and legs and extract the meat. Turn the crab shell over and press up with thumbs to push out the underbody. Cut this piece in quarters and use a skewer to pick out the meat. Discard the stomach sac and the lungs (dead man's fingers). Set the white meat aside with the claw meat. Using a teaspoon, scrape out the brown meat from inside the shell and reserve it. If the roe is present reserve that, too.

Melt the butter or margarine in a medium saucepan and soften the onion for about 3 minutes. Do not allow to brown. Stir in the flour and milk. Bring to the boil and then immediately turn down the heat to simmer. Add the brown meat from the crab and cook gently for about 20 minutes. Add the sherry, salt, pepper, mace, white crab meat and roe. Cook a further 5 minutes.

Top each serving with a spoonful of whipped cream and red caviar.

Top: vacationers enjoy the Cypress Gardens at Charleston, South Carolina.

Oregano Oysters

Preparation Time: 25 minutes **Cooking Time:** 20-25 minutes **Serves:** 4

The combination of oregano and the anise taste of Pernod is an unusual but very complementary one, especially with fresh oysters.

Ingredients
1 tbsp butter or margarine
1 clove garlic, crushed
1 tbsp chopped parsley
1 tbsp chopped fresh oregano or
   dried oregano
1 tbsp Pernod

¾ cup heavy cream
Salt and pepper
24 oysters on the half shell
12 strips bacon, cooked and crumbled
Coarse salt

Melt the butter or margarine in a saucepan. Add the garlic and cook to soften, but do not brown. Add the parsley, oregano, Pernod and cream. Bring to the boil and lower the heat to simmering. Strain on any liquid from the oysters and then loosen them from their shells with a small, sharp knife. Cook the mixture until reduced by about one quarter and slightly thickened. Add the seasoning and set the mixture aside. Pour about 1 inch coarse salt into a baking pan. Place the oysters on top of the salt and twist the shells into the salt so that they stand level. Spoon some of the cream over each oyster and sprinkle with the crumbled bacon. Bake in a pre-heated 400°F oven for 15-18 minutes. Serve immediately.

Top: an elegant mansion in Alabama provides the perfect setting for an *al fresco* dinner.

Sea Island Shrimp

Preparation Time: 30 minutes **Cooking Time:** 15 minutes **Serves:** 2-4

Although this is a recipe from the Carolinas, it is popular everywhere succulent shrimp are available.

Ingredients

2 dozen raw large shrimp, unpeeled
4 tbsps butter or margarine
1 small red pepper, seeded and finely chopped
2 green onions, finely chopped
½ tsp dry mustard
2 tsps dry sherry
1 tsp Worcester sauce

4oz cooked crab meat
6 tbsps fresh breadcrumbs
1 tbsp chopped parsley
2 tbsps mayonnaise
Salt and pepper
1 small egg, beaten
Grated Parmesan cheese
Paprika

Remove all of the shrimp shells except for the very tail ends. Remove the black veins on the rounded sides. Cut the shrimp down the length of the curved side and press each one open.

Melt half the butter or margarine in a small pan and cook the pepper to soften – about 3 minutes. Add the green onions and cook a further 2 minutes. Combine the red pepper and green onion with the mustard, sherry, Worcester sauce, crab meat, breadcrumbs, parsley and mayonnaise. Add seasoning and enough egg to bind together. Spoon the stuffing onto the shrimp and sprinkle with the Parmesan cheese and the paprika. Melt the remaining butter or margarine and drizzle over the shrimp. Bake in a pre-heated 350°F oven for about 10 minutes. Serve immediately.

Edisto Beach in South Carolina is a tranquil haven during the quiet winter months.

Snapper with Fennel and Orange Salad

Preparation Time: 30 minutes **Cooking Time:** 6-10 minutes **Serves:** 4

Red snapper brings Florida to mind. Combined with oranges, it makes a lovely summer meal.

Ingredients

Oil
4 even-sized red snapper, cleaned, heads and tails on
2 heads fennel

2 oranges
Juice of 1 lemon
3 tbsps light salad oil
Pinch sugar, salt and black pepper

Brush both sides of the fish with oil and cut three slits in the sides of each. Sprinkle with a little of the lemon juice, reserving the rest. Slice the fennel in half and remove the cores. Slice thinly. Also slice the green tops and chop the feathery herb to use in the dressing. Peel the oranges, removing all the white pith. Cut the oranges into segments. Peel and segment over a bowl to catch the juice. Add lemon juice to any orange juice collected in the bowl. Add the salad oil, salt, pepper and a pinch of sugar, if necessary. Mix well and add the fennel, green herb tops and orange segments, stirring carefully. Broil the fish 3-5 minutes per side, depending on thickness. Serve the fish with heads and tails on, accompanied by the salad.

Top: the ancient tugboat *John Taxis* stands above the waters of the Cape Fear River.

River Inn Quail

Preparation Time: 25 minutes **Cooking Time:** 45-50 minutes **Serves:** 4

Definitely a dish for special occasions, this is deceptively simple, impressive and perfect for entertaining.

Ingredients

12 dressed quail
6 tbsps butter
3 tbsps oil
1 clove garlic, crushed
4oz mushrooms, sliced
4 tbsps chopped pecans or walnuts
4 tbsps raisins

1 cup chicken stock
Salt and pepper
3 tbsps sherry
1 tbsp cornstarch
1 tsp tomato paste (optional)
1 bunch watercress

Rub each quail inside and out with butter. Pour the oil into a baking pan large enough to hold the quail comfortably. Cook in a pre-heated 350°F oven for about 25 minutes, uncovered. Remove the pan from the oven and place under a pre-heated broiler to brown the quail. Add garlic, mushrooms, pecans, raisins and stock to the quail. Replace in the oven and continue to cook, uncovered, until the quail are tender – a further 20 minutes. Remove the quail and the other ingredients to a serving dish, leaving the pan juices behind. Mix the cornstarch and sherry and add it to the pan, stirring constantly. Place the pan over medium heat and cook until the cornstarch thickens and clears. If the baking pan isn't flameproof, transfer the ingredients to a saucepan before thickening the sauce. Add the tomato paste, if necessary, for color. Pour the sauce over the quail and garnish with watercress to serve.

Top: fishing on the waterfront at New Bern, the second oldest city in North Carolina.

Jekyll Island Shrimp

Preparation Time: 35-40 minutes **Cooking Time:** 20 minutes **Serves:** 2-4

Named for an island off the Georgia coast, this makes a rich appetizer or an elegant main course.

Ingredients

2lbs cooked shrimp	6 tbsps fine dry breadcrumbs
4 tbsps butter, softened	2 tbsps chopped parsley
Pinch salt, white pepper and cayenne	4 tbsps sherry
1 clove garlic, crushed	Lemon wedges or slices

To prepare the shrimp, remove the heads and legs first. Peel off the shells, carefully removing the tail shells. Remove the black vein running down the length of the rounded side with a wooden pick. Arrange shrimp in a shallow casserole or individual dishes.

Combine the remaining ingredients, except the lemon garnish, mixing well. Spread the mixture to completely cover the shrimp and place in a pre-heated 375°F oven for about 20 minutes, or until the butter melts and the crumbs become crisp. Garnish with lemon wedges or slices.

Fishing boats at Dauphin Island near Mobile, Alabama's only large port.

Fried Chicken

Preparation Time: 20 minutes **Cooking Time:** 25 minutes **Serves:** 4

No discussion of Southern cooking is complete without mentioning fried chicken. Eating it is even better than talking about it.

Ingredients

3lb frying chicken portions	½ tsp black pepper
2 eggs	Pinch cayenne pepper (optional)
2 cups flour	Oil for frying
1 tsp each salt, paprika and sage	Parsley or watercress

Rinse chicken and pat dry. Beat the eggs in a large bowl and add the chicken one piece at a time, turning to coat. Mix flour and seasonings in a large paper or plastic bag. Place chicken pieces coated with egg into the bag one at a time, close bag tightly and shake to coat each piece of chicken. Alternatively, dip each coated chicken piece in a bowl of seasoned flour, shaking of the excess.

Heat oil in a large frying pan to the depth of about ½ inch. When oil is hot, add the chicken skin side down first. Fry for about 12 minutes and then turn over. Fry a further 12 minutes or until juices run clear. Drain chicken on paper towels and serve immediately. Garnish serving plate with parsley or watercress.

Green tomatoes fried in butter and lightly seasoned are a tasty Southern favorite.

Brunswick Stew

Preparation Time: 1 hour **Cooking Time:** 2 hours **Serves:** 6-8

Peppers, potatoes, corn, tomatoes, onions and lima beans are staple ingredients in this recipe, which often includes squirrel in its really authentic version.

Ingredients

3lbs chicken portions
6 tbsps flour
3 tbsps butter or margarine
8oz salt pork, rinded and cut into ¼ inch dice
3 medium onions, finely chopped
3 pints water
3 14oz cans tomatoes
3 tbsps tomato paste
4oz fresh or frozen lima beans

4oz corn
2 large red peppers, seeded and cut into small dice
3 medium potatoes, peeled and cut into ½ inch cubes
Salt and pepper
1-2 tsps cayenne pepper or Tabasco, or to taste
2 tsps Worcester sauce
1 cup red wine

Shake the pieces of chicken in the flour in a plastic bag as for Fried Chicken. In a large, deep sauté pan, melt the butter until foaming. Place in the chicken without crowding the pieces and brown over moderately high heat for about 10-12 minutes. Remove the chicken and set it aside. In the same pan, fry the salt pork until the fat is rendered and the dice are crisp. Add the onions and cook over a moderate heat for about 10 minutes, or until softened but not browned.

Pour the water into a large stockpot or saucepan and spoon in the onions, pork and any meat juices from the pan. Add the chicken, tomatoes and tomato paste. Bring to the boil, reduce the heat and simmer for about 1-1½ hours. Add the lima beans, corn, peppers and potatoes. Add the cayenne pepper or Tabasco to taste. Add the Worcester sauce and red wine. Cook for a further 30 minutes or until the chicken is tender. Add salt and pepper to taste.

The stew should be rather thick, so if there is too much liquid, remove the chicken and vegetables and boil down the liquid to reduce it. If there is not enough liquid, add more water or chicken stock.

Alabama Cola Glazed Ham

Preparation Time: 30 minutes plus overnight soaking
Cooking Time: 2 hours 15 minutes **Serves:** 8-10

Don't be afraid to try this somewhat unusual approach to roast ham. Cola gives it a marvelous taste and color.

Ingredients

10lb joint country or Smithfield ham	Whole cloves
4 cups cola soft drink	1 cup packed dark brown sugar

Soak the ham overnight. Preheat oven to 350°F. Place the ham rind side down in a roasting pan. Pour over all but 6 tbsps of the cola and bake, uncovered, 1½ hours or until the internal temperature registers 140°F. Baste the ham every 20 minutes with the pan juices using a large spoon or bulb baster. Remove the ham from the oven and allow it to cool for 10-15 minutes. Remove the rind from the ham with a small, sharp knife and score the fat to a depth of ¼ inch. Stick 1 clove in the center of every other diamond. Mix sugar and the remaining cola together and pour or spread over the ham. Raise the oven temperature to 375°F. Return the ham to the oven and bake for 45 minutes, basting every 15 minutes. Cover loosely with foil if the ham begins to brown too much. Allow to stand 15 minutes before slicing.

Top: Oak Alley Plantation, built in 1850, is one of the South's most famous grand homes.

Cornish Hens with Southern Stuffing

Preparation Time: 45-50 minutes **Cooking Time:** about 1 hour **Serves:** 6

Cornbread makes a delicious stuffing and a change from the usual breadcrumb variations.

Ingredients

Full quantity Corn Muffin recipe
2 tbsps butter or margarine
2 sticks celery, finely chopped
2 green onions, chopped
2oz chopped country or
   Smithfield ham

2oz chopped pecans
Salt and pepper
2 tbsps bourbon
1 egg, beaten
6 Cornish game hens
12 strips bacon

Prepare the corn muffins according to the recipe, allow to cool completely and crumble finely. Melt the butter or margarine and soften the celery and onions for about 5 minutes over very low heat. Add the ham, pecans, cornbread crumbs and seasoning. Add bourbon and just enough egg to make a stuffing that holds together but is not too wet. Remove the giblets from the hens, if included, and fill each bird with stuffing. Sew up the cavity with fine string or close with small skewers. Criss-cross 2 strips of bacon over the breasts of each bird and tie or skewer the ends of the bacon together. Roast in a pre-heated 400°F oven for 45 minutes - 1 hour, or until tender. Baste the hens with the pan juices as they cook. Remove the bacon, if desired, during the last 15 minutes to brown the breasts, or serve with the bacon after removing the string or skewers.

Storm clouds gather over the fertile farmlands of Georgia.

Lamb Parcels

Preparation Time: 30 minutes **Cooking Time:** 45 minutes - 1 hour **Serves:** 2

This simple recipe makes a whole meal in one convenient parcel.

Ingredients

2 lamb steaks or 4 rib chops
Oil
1 large potato, scrubbed
4 baby carrots, scraped
1 medium onion, peeled and sliced

1 medium green pepper, seeded
   and sliced
1 tbsp chopped fresh dill
Salt and pepper

Heat a frying pan and add a small amount of oil. Quickly fry the lamb on both sides to sear and brown. Cut 2 pieces of foil about 12 x 18". Lightly oil the foil. Cut the potatoes in half and place half on each piece of foil, cut side up. Top with the lamb and place the carrots on either side. Place the onion slices on the lamb and the pepper slices on top of the onions. Sprinkle with dill, salt and pepper, and seal into parcels. Bake at 400°F for about 45 minutes-1 hour, or until the potatoes are tender and the meat is cooked. Open the parcels at the table.

A traditional-style restaurant in Tennessee offers a warm welcome to passing tourists.

Country Captain Chicken

Preparation Time: 30 minutes **Cooking Time:** about 50 minutes **Serves:** 6

A flavorful dish named for a sea captain with a taste for the spicy cuisine of India.

Ingredients

3lbs chicken portions
Seasoned flour
6 tbsps oil
1 medium onion, chopped
1 medium green pepper, seeded
   and chopped
1 clove garlic, crushed

Pinch salt and pepper
2 tsps curry powder
2 14oz cans tomatoes
2 tsps chopped parsley
1 tsp chopped marjoram
4 tbsps currants or raisins
4oz blanched almond halves

Remove skin from the chicken and dredge with flour, shaking off the excess. Heat the oil and brown the chicken on all sides until golden. Remove to an ovenproof casserole. Pour off all but 2 tbsps of the oil. Add the onion, pepper and garlic and cook slowly to soften. Add the seasonings and curry powder and cook, stirring frequently, for 2 minutes. Add the tomatoes, parsley, majoram and bring to the boil. Pour the sauce over the chicken, cover and cook in a pre-heated 350°F oven for 45 minutes. Add the currants or raisins during the last 15 minutes.

Meanwhile, toast the almonds in the oven on a cookie sheet along with the chicken. Stir them carefully and watch carefully. Sprinkle over the chicken just before serving.

Cotton plants gradually encroach on an old, abandoned farmhouse in Alabama.

Broiled Flounder

Preparation Time: 25 minutes **Cooking Time:** 9-15 minutes **Serves:** 4

A mayonnaise-like topping puffs to a golden brown to give this mild-flavored fish a piquant taste.

Ingredients

4 double fillets of flounder	4 tbsps pickle relish
2 eggs, separated	1 tbsp chopped parsley
Pinch salt, pepper and dry mustard	1 tbsp lemon juice
1 cup peanut oil	Dash Tabasco

Place the egg yolks in a blender, food processor or deep bowl. Blend in the salt, pepper and mustard. If blending by hand, use a small whisk. If using the machine, pour the oil through the funnel in a thin, steady stream with the machine running. If mixing by hand, add oil a few drops at a time, beating well in between each addition. When half the oil has been added, the rest may be added in a thin steady stream while beating constantly with a small whisk. Mix in the relish, parsley, lemon juice and Tabasco. Beat the egg whites until stiff but not dry and fold into the mayonnaise.

Broil the fish about 2 inches from the heat source for about 6-10 minutes, depending on the thickness of the fillets. Spread the sauce over each fillet and broil 3-5 minutes longer, or until the sauce puffs and browns lightly.

Azaleas bring a blaze of color to a cool, peaceful corner of South Carolina.

Country Ham with Bourbon Raisin Sauce

Preparation Time: about 30 minutes **Cooking Time:** 10-15 minutes
Serves: 4-8

The tart and sweet flavor of this sauce has long been the choice to complement savory country ham.

Ingredients
8 slices country or Smithfield ham,
   cut about ¼ inch thick
Milk
Oil or margarine for frying

Sauce
1½ tbsps cornstarch
1 cup apple cider
½ tsp ginger or allspice
2 tsps lemon juice
2 tbsps bourbon
2oz raisins
Pinch salt

Soak the ham slices in enough milk to barely cover for at least 30 minutes. Rinse and pat dry. Trim off the rind and discard it. Heat a small amount of oil or margarine in a large frying pan and brown the ham slices about 2 minutes per side over medium-high heat. Mix the cornstarch with about 6 tbsps of the apple cider and deglaze the frying pan with the remaining cider. Stir in the ginger or allspice and the lemon juice. Stirring constantly, pour in the cornstarch mixture and bring the liquid to the boil. Cook and stir constantly until thickened. Add the bourbon and raisins and cook a further 5 minutes. Add salt to taste. Reheat the ham quickly, if necessary, and pour over the sauce to serve.

Top: a cool spot on the bayou provides the perfect setting for a refreshing picnic.

Jellied Avocado Salad

Preparation Time: 25 minutes **Cooking Time:** 2 hours to set **Serves:** 4-6

Salads set with gelatin are cooling treats in summer or perfect do-ahead dishes anytime.

Ingredients

Juice of 1 small lemon
1½ tbsps unflavored gelatin
2 ripe avocados
3oz cream cheese or low fat
   soft cheese

½ cup sour cream or natural yogurt
2 tbsps mayonnaise
3 oranges, peeled and segmented
Flat Italian parsley or coriander
   to garnish

Reserve about 2 tsps of the lemon juice. Pour the rest into a small dish, sprinkle the gelatin on top and allow to stand until spongy. Cut the avocados in half and twist to separate. Reserve half of one avocado with the stone attached and brush the cut surface with lemon juice, wrap in plastic wrap and keep in the refrigerator. Remove the stone from the other half and scrape the pulp from the three halves into a food processor. Add the cheese, sour cream or yogurt and mayonnaise and process until smooth.

Melt the gelatin and add it to the avocado mixture with the machine running. Place a small disc of wax paper in custard cups, oil the sides of the cups and the paper and pour in the mixture. Tap the cups lightly on a flat surface to smooth the top and eliminate any air bubbles, cover with plastic wrap and chill until set. Loosen the set mixture carefully form the sides of the cups and invert each onto a serving plate to unmold.

Peel and slice the remaining avocado half and use to decorate the plate along with the orange segments. Place parsley or coriander leaves on top of each avocado mold to serve.

Cabbage and Peanut Slaw

Preparation Time: 30 minutes **Serves:** 6

Boiled dressings are old favorites in the South. This one gives a lively sweet-sour taste to basic coleslaw.

Ingredients

1 small head white or red cabbage, or mixture, finely shredded
2 carrots, shredded
2 tsps celery seed
1 cup dry-roasted peanuts

1 egg
½ cup white wine vinegar
½ cup water
½ tsp dry mustard
2 tbsps sugar

Combine the vegetables, celery seed and peanuts in a large bowl. Beat the egg in a small bowl. Add vinegar, water, mustard and sugar and blend thoroughly. Place the bowl in a pan of very hot water and whisk until thickened. Cool and pour over the vegetables.

A neat row of buildings in the grounds of Wake Forest University, Winston-Salem, North Carolina.

Minted Mixed Vegetables

Preparation Time: 25-30 minutes **Cooking Time:** 6-10 minutes **Serves:** 4-6

Carrots, cucumber and zucchini are all complemented by the taste of fresh mint. In fact, most vegetables are, so experiment.

Ingredients

3 medium carrots
1 cucumber
2 zucchini
½ cup water
1 tsp sugar

Pinch salt
1½ tbsps butter, cut into small pieces
1 tbsp coarsely chopped fresh
    mint leaves

Peel the carrots and cut them into sticks about ½ inch thick and 2½ inches long. Peel the cucumber and cut it into quarters, remove the centers and cut into sticks the same size as the carrots. Cut the zucchini into sticks the same size as the other vegetables. Combine the carrots, water, sugar and salt in a medium saucepan. Cover the pan and bring to the boil over high heat. Reduce the heat to medium and cook for about 3 minutes. Uncover the pan and cook a further 3 minutes. Increase the heat and add the cucumber and zucchini and boil until the vegetables are tender-crisp. Add the butter and stir over heat until melted and the liquid has completely evaporated, glazing the vegetables. Remove from the heat, add the mint and toss well.

Top: with the arrival of summer, crowds flock to Daytona Beach in Florida.

Quick Fried Vegetables with Herbs

Preparation Time: 25 minutes **Cooking Time:** 5 minutes **Serves:** 6

Crisply cooked vegetables with plenty of chives make a perfect side dish, hot or cold.

Ingredients

4 sticks celery
3-4 tbsps oil
4 medium zucchini
2 red peppers, seeded

Pinch salt and pepper
1 tsp chopped fresh oregano
  or marjoram
4 tbsps snipped fresh chives

Slice the celery on the diagonal into pieces about 1½ inches thick. Cut the zucchini in half lengthwise and then cut into ½ inch thick slices. Remove all the seeds and white pith from the peppers and cut them into diagonal pieces about 1 inch. Heat the oil in a heavy frying pan over medium-high heat. Add the celery and stir-fry until barely tender. Add zucchini and peppers and stir-fry until all the vegetables are tender-crisp. Add salt, pepper and oregano or marjoram and cook for 30 seconds more. Stir in chives and serve immediately.

The general store in Louisiana State University's Rural Life Museum.

Fried Okra

Preparation Time: 15-20 minutes **Cooking Time:** 3 minutes per batch
Serves: 4-6

Cornmeal and okra, two Southern specialties, combine in a classic vegetable
dish that's delicious with meat, poultry, game or fish.

Ingredients
1 cup yellow cornmeal
1 tsp salt
2 eggs, beaten
1½lbs fresh okra, washed, stemmed
    and cut crosswise into ½ inch
    thick slices
2 cups oil for frying

Combine the cornmeal and salt on a plate. Coat okra pieces in beaten egg.
Dredge the okra in the mixture. Place the oil in a large, deep sauté pan and
place over moderate heat. When the temperature reaches 375°F add the okra
in batches and fry until golden brown. Drain thoroughly on paper towels and
serve immediately.

The golden glow of the setting sun signals the onset of evening in the swamplands
of Alabama.

Sweet Potato Pudding

Preparation Time: 25 minutes **Cooking Time:** 45 minutes-1 hour **Serves:** 6

All puddings are not necessarily desserts. This one goes with meat or poultry for an unusual side dish.

Ingredients
2 medium-sized sweet potatoes
2 cups milk
2 eggs
¾ cup sugar

1 tsp cinnamon
¼ cup pecans, roughly chopped
2 tbsps butter
6 tbsps bourbon

Peel the potatoes and grate them coarsely. Combine with the milk. Beat the eggs and gradually add the sugar, continuing until light and fluffy. Combine with the cinnamon and the pecans. Stir into the potatoes and milk and pour the mixture into a lightly buttered shallow baking dish. Dot with the remaining butter. Bake about 45 minutes to 1 hour in a pre-heated 350°F oven. Bake until the pudding is set and then pour over the bourbon just before serving.

Top: the pace of life in rural Georgia is slow, and picking home-grown vegetables is a pleasure still enjoyed by those who prepare Georgia's famous country food.

Lemon Chess Pie

Preparation Time: 30 minutes **Cooking Time:** 45 minutes **Serves:** 6

No one is really sure how this zesty lemon and cornmeal pie came to be so named, but it's delicious nonetheless.

Ingredients

1½ cups all-purpose flour
Pinch salt and sugar
6 tbsps butter or margarine
2 tbsps plus 1 tsp vegetable
   shortening
4-5 tbsps cold water

Filling
4 tbsps softened butter
1 cup sugar
3-4 eggs, depending on size
1 tbsp yellow cornmeal
Rind and juice of 1 lemon

Sift the flour, salt and sugar into a bowl or process once or twice in a food processor. Add the butter or margarine and shortening and rub into the flour until the mixture resembles fine breadcrumbs, or use a food processor. Add enough water to bring the mixture together in a firm dough. Knead lightly to eliminate cracks, wrap and chill for 30 minutes while preparing the filling.

Cream the butter with the sugar until the sugar dissolves. Add the eggs, one at a time, beating well in between each addition. Stir in the cornmeal, rind and juice of the lemon. Roll out the pastry in a circle on a well-floured surface. Roll the pastry carefully onto the rolling pin and transfer to a 9-inch pie or flan dish. Lower the pastry carefully into the dish and press against the sides and base. Trim the edges with a sharp knife if using a pie dish, or roll over the rim of the flan dish with the rolling pin to cut off the excess. Pour in the filling and bake at 350°F for about 45 minutes. Lower the temperature to 325°F if the pie begins to brown too quickly. Cook until the filling sets. Allow to cool completely before serving. Sprinkle lightly with powdered sugar before cutting, if desired.

Top: fertile farmlands in North Carolina.

Stained Glass Dessert

Preparation Time: 35-40 minutes **Cooking Time:** 1-1½ hours to set and overnight refrigeration **Serves:** 6-8

Named for the effect of the cubes of colorful gelatin in the filling, this pretty and light pudding can be made well in advance of serving.

Ingredients

3oz each of three fruit-flavored gelatin (assorted)	4 tbsps cold water
2 cups graham crackers, crushed	3 eggs, separated
6 tbsps sugar	6 tbsps sugar
½ cup butter or margarine	4oz cream cheese
3 tbsps unflavored gelatin	Juice and rind of 1 large lemon
	½ cup whipping cream

Prepare the flavored gelatins according to package directions. Pour into 3 shallow pans and refrigerate until firm.

Mix the crushed graham crackers with the sugar in a food processor. Pour melted butter thorough the funnel with the machine running to blend thoroughly. Press half the mixture into an 8 inch springform pan lined with wax paper. Refrigerate until firm. Reserve half the mixture for topping. Sprinkle the gelatin onto the water in a small saucepan and allow to stand until spongy. Heat gently until the gelatin dissolves and the liquid is clear. Combine the egg yolks, lemon juice and sugar and beat until slightly thickened. Beat in the cream cheese a bit at a time. Pour in the gelatin in a thin, steady stream, beating constantly. Allow to stand, stirring occasionally until beginning to thicken. Place in a bowl of ice water to speed up the setting process. Whip the cream until soft. Whip the egg whites until stiff peaks form and fold both the cream and egg whites into the lemon-cream cheese mixture when the gelatin has begun to thicken. Cut the flavored gelatins into cubes and fold carefully into the cream cheese mixture. Pour onto the prepared crust. Sprinkle the remaining crust mixture on top, pressing down very carefully. Chill overnight in the refrigerator. Loosen the mixture carefully from the sides of the pan, open the pan and unmold. Slice or spoon out to serve.

Strawberry Shortcake

Preparation Time: 30-35 minutes **Cooking Time:** 15 minutes **Serves:** 6

Summer wouldn't be the same without strawberry shortcake. Add a liqueur to the fruit for a slightly sophisticated touch.

Ingredients

2 cups all-purpose flour	⅓-½ cup milk
1 tbsp baking powder	Melted butter
Pinch salt	1lb fresh or frozen strawberries
3 tbsps sugar	Powdered sugar
6 tbsps cream cheese, softened	Juice of half an orange
3 tbsps butter or margarine	4 tbsps Eau de Fraises or orange liqueur
1 egg, beaten	1 cup whipped cream

Sift the flour, baking powder, salt and sugar into a large bowl. Using 2 knives, forks or a pastry blender, cut in the cheese and butter or margarine. A food processor can also be used. Blend in the egg and enough milk to make a firm dough. Knead lightly on a floured surface and then roll out to a thickness of ½ inch. Cut the dough into an even number of 3 inch circles. Re-roll the trimmings and cut as before. Brush half of the circles with the melted butter and place the other halves on top, pressing down lightly. Bake on an ungreased cookie sheet for about 15 minutes in a pre-heated 425°F oven. Allow to cool slightly and then transfer to a wire rack.

Hull the strawberries and wash well. Purée half of them in a food processor with the orange juice and liqueur. Add powdered sugar to taste if desired. Cut the remaining strawberries in half and combine with the purée. Separate the shortcakes in half and place the bottoms on serving plates. Spoon over the strawberries and sauce and pipe or spoon on the cream. Sprinkle the tops of the shortcake with powdered sugar and place on top of the cream. Serve slightly warm or at room temperature.

Southern Biscuits

Preparation Time: 20 minutes **Cooking Time:** 10-12 minutes **Makes:** 6-8

Hot biscuits with butter and sometimes honey are a symbol of Southern cooking, for breakfast, lunch, dinner or all three!

Ingredients

1¾ cups all-purpose flour
½ tsp salt
2 tsps baking powder
1 tsp sugar

½ tsp baking soda
5 tbsps margarine or 4 tbsps
    shortening
¾ cup buttermilk

Sift the flour, salt, baking powder, sugar and baking soda into a large bowl. Rub in the fat until the mixture resembles coarse crumbs. Mix in enough buttermilk to form a soft dough. It may not be necessary to use all the milk. Turn the dough out onto a floured surface and knead lightly until smooth. Roll the dough out on a floured surface to a thickness of ½-¾ inch. Cut into rounds with a 2½ inch cookie cutter. Place the circles of dough on a lightly-greased cookie sheet about 1 inch apart. Bake in a pre-heated 450°F oven for 10-12 minutes. Serve hot.

Top: a costumed docent relaxes after a hard day's baking in the reconstructed kitchen of an old cottage in Rose Hill State Park near Union.

Pecan Tassies

Preparation Time: 25 minutes plus 1 hour chilling **Cooking Time:** 20 minutes
Makes: 24

Like miniature pecan pies, these small pastries are popular throughout the Southern states, especially at Christmas.

Ingredients
Pastry
½ cup butter or margarine
6 tbsps cream cheese
1 cup all-purpose flour

Filling
¾ cup chopped pecans
1 egg
¾ cup packed light brown sugar
1 tbsp softened butter
1 tsp vanilla extract
Powdered sugar

Beat the butter or margarine and cheese together to soften. Stir in the flour, adding more if necessary to make the dough easy to handle, although it will still be soft. If possible, roll the dough into 1 inch balls. Chill thoroughly on a plate.

Mix all the filling ingredients together thoroughly, omitting the powdered sugar. Place a ball of chilled dough into a small tart pan and, with floured fingers, press up the sides and over the base of the pans. Repeat with all the balls of dough. Spoon in the filling and bake for about 20-25 minutes at 350°F. Allow to cool about 5 minutes and remove carefully from the pans. Cool completely on a wire rack before sprinkling with powdered sugar.

At one time it was mainly cargo that the ferry boats carried. Today it is vacationers.

Corn Muffins

Preparation Time: 20 minutes **Cooking Time:** about 15 minutes **Makes:** 12

A cross between cake and bread, these muffins are slightly sweet and crumbly. Originally a Native American recipe, they've become typically Southern.

Ingredients

1 cup all-purpose flour	1 cup yellow cornmeal
4 tbsps sugar	1 egg, slightly beaten
2 tsps baking powder	4 tbsps oil
½ tsp salt	1⅓ cups milk

Pre-heat the oven to 450°F. Grease a muffin pan liberally with oil. Heat the pan for 5 minutes in the oven. Sift the flour, sugar, baking powder and salt into a large bowl. Add the cornmeal and stir to blend, leaving a well in the center. Combine the egg, oil and milk and pour into the well. Beat with a wooden spoon, gradually incorporating the dry ingredients into the liquid. Do not overbeat the mixture. It can be lumpy. Spoon the batter into the pans and bake for about 14 minutes. Cool briefly in the pans and then remove to a wire rack to cool further. Serve warm.

Country music fans find an endless supply of willing entertainers in Tennessee.

Lemonade

Preparation Time: 20 minutes **Makes:** 5 cups

Nothing surpasses a cold glass of lemonade in the summer. This is the essential beverage for picnics and barbecues.

Ingredients
1 lemon
¾ cup sugar
4½ cups water

Maraschino cherries
Lemon slices

Wash the lemon well and cut into small pieces, removing the seeds. Place in a blender or food processor with the sugar and 1 cup water. Blend until smooth, add remaining water and mix well. Pour into ice-filled glasses or into a pitcher filled with ice and garnish with the cherries and lemon slices.

Top: the evocative architecture of Sir Walter Raleigh Street in Manteo, one of the largest towns on Roanoke Island.

Mint Julep

Preparation Time: about 15-20 minutes **Makes:** 1 drink

The official drink of the Kentucky Derby, it's mint and bourbon with a splash of soda – delicious but potent.

Ingredients
2 shots bourbon   1 tsp sugar
3 sprigs of fresh mint   Soda or carbonated mineral water

Place 1 sprig of mint into a bowl, glass or jug and crush thoroughly with the sugar. Add ⅓-¼ cup of soda or mineral water, mash again and add the bourbon. Pour the mixture through a strainer into a tall glass filled with crushed ice. Stir until the glass frosts, or leave in the refrigerator about 5 minutes. Decorate the glass with the remaining sprigs of mint.

Many of the South's family homes are reminiscent of elegant plantation houses.

Alabama Cola Glazed Ham 30
Appetizers and Soups:
Virginia Peanut Soup 10
Corn and Potato Chowder 12
She Crab Soup 14
Oregano Oysters 16
Sea Island Shrimp 18
Broiled Flounder 38
Brunswick Stew 28
Cabbage and Peanut Slaw 44
Cakes and Desserts:
Corn Muffins 64
Lemon Chess Pie 54
Pecan Tassies 62
Southern Biscuits 60
Stained Glass Dessert 56
Strawberry Shortcake 58
Sweet Potato Pudding 52
Corn and Potato Chowder 12
Corn Muffins 64
Cornish Hens with Southern Stuffing 32
Country Captain Chicken 36
Country Ham with Bourbon Raisin Sauce 40
Drinks:
Lemonade 66
Mint Julep 68
Fish and Seafood:
Broiled Flounder 38
Jekyll Island Shrimp 24
Snapper with Fennel and Orange
Salad 20
Fried Chicken 26
Fried Okra 50
Jekyll Island Shrimp 24
Jellied Avocado Salad 42

Lamb Parcels 34
Lemonade 66
Lemon Chess Pie 54
Meat Dishes:
Alabama Cola Glazed Ham 30
Brunswick Stew 28
Country Ham with Bourbon Raisin
Sauce 40
Lamb Parcels 34
Mint Julep 68
Minted Mixed Vegetables 46
Oregano Oysters 16
Pecan Tassies 62
Poultry and Game:
Cornish Hens with Southern
Stuffing 32
Country Captain Chicken 36
Fried Chicken 26
River Inn Quail 22
Quick Fried Vegetables 48
River Inn Quail 22
Sea Island Shrimp 18
She Crab Soup 14
Side Dishes and Salads:
Cabbage and Peanut Slaw 44
Fried Okra 50
Jellied Avocado Salad 42
Minted Mixed Vegetables 46
Quick Fried Vegetables 48
Snapper with Fennel and Orange Salad 20
Southern Biscuits 60
Stained Glass Dessert 56
Strawberry Shortcake 58
Sweet Potato Pudding 52
Virginia Peanut Soup 10